TASTE AND SMELL!

Can·Make·and·Do Books

TASTE AND SMELL!

40 Tasting and Smelling Experiences for Children, Plus 60 Recipes to Cook, Eat, and Drink

by Joy Wilt
Terre Watson

Photography by Terry Staus

CREATIVE RESOURCES
Waco, Texas

Acknowledgements

We would like to thank some very special people for their ideas and help we received in producing this book:

    Terry Staus, a very talented photographer

    Melena Edmonston, a great cook and editor

    Connie Vandenberg, our editor

    Casey and Traci Augulis and Ginger and Melody Stewart, four delightful children who tasted and smelled their way through most of our book.

With the help of these friends we have been able to share our ideas with you. Enjoy!

JOY WILT

TERRE WATSON

Contents

The Importance of Sensory Experiences

This book is one of a series of four books about SENSORY EXPERIENCES FOR CHILDREN. This book deals with TASTING AND SMELLING experiences, while the other three books deal with:

TACTILE experiences
VISUAL experiences
LISTENING experiences.

We have chosen to devote four entire books to sensory experience because we feel that these experiences for children are very important.

Why are sensory experiences so important?
Because *ALL LEARNING AND COMMUNICATION BEGINS WITH SENSORY EXPERIENCES.*

A child is born "fully equipped" with a set of "natural tools"—the senses of sound, touch, sight, taste, and smell. These tools enable him to explore and discover the world of which he is a part. Exploration and discovery are vital to a child's life because they lead him into growth and development.

Each of the four sensory experience books is packed full of suggested experiences—experiences that are designed to

—assist a child in becoming *aware* of his senses
—encourage a child to *develop* his senses

9

—give a child the opportunity to begin using his senses as tools to answer his questions and *educate* himself
—allow a child to *enjoy* life through his senses.

The sensory experiences that we recommend can be the exciting beginning of a child's understanding and enjoyment of his world. They can be the foundation for every learning experience the child will ever encounter. They can make learning a relevant part of every child's life.

This is why we believe that sensory experiences in general should not be an "optional part" of any program. Indeed, they should be an integral part.

The particular experiences that we have chosen have been tested and found to be successful with
—infants
—toddlers
—preschoolers
—children 6–12 years of age

Each experience can be adapted to fit into any situation at
—home
—school
—church
—social functions
—recreational programs

Each sensory experience can be experienced by an individual child or by a group of children.

No matter what particular sensory experience is used, how it is used, or where it is used, it has great potential for bringing children of all ages in touch with themselves and their world.

About Tasting and Smelling Experiences

This book specializes in tasting and smelling experiences for children. We have written an entire book about these two senses because we feel they add a marvelous dimension to a child's everyday experience.

When a child encounters something that he cannot see, touch, or hear, he moves from the concrete to the intangible. Smelling can be a child's first experience with symbolization. For example, smells mean different things to every child. The smell of peppermint may remind one child of Christmas while another may think of medicine. The smell of roses may remind one child of funerals while another may think of weddings. A smell can excite a whole train of thought. It can stimulate the imagination. It can motivate a child to explore. Indeed, smelling can be an important part of a child's creative, intellectual, and educational experience.

When asked what they enjoyed most about a party or other special occasion, many children will reply, "The refreshments!" Needless to say, eating is a pleasurable experience. Pleasure is one reason to develop a child's sense of taste, but another more important reason is survival. Children must eat to survive, and the diet they consume must include more than junk food and candy.

This book strives to bring children into a greater understanding and appreciation of the whole gamut of taste. It encourages children to develop a taste for all foods. So that a balanced diet will be eaten and enjoyed, we have included many recipes, any of which children can prepare themselves.

We think it is strategic for children to cook their own food because then and only then can they begin to understand the process. Casseroles become less foreboding when children see firsthand what the casserole consists of. Applesauce makes more sense when they can watch the apples change through cooking. Children can really begin to understand what is meant by "Lemonade comes from lemons." In addition, we have found that children will eat almost anything that they prepare themselves (mud pies are proof of this), so the sky's the limit when it comes to introducing children to new foods.

Cooking obviously can add to a language, science, or math lesson in a way that no other experience can. And in the socialization process, we have found that nothing brings a group together better than cooking for each other and eating together.

You can't lose! Try it—you'll like it!

Smell Experiences

Paper Bag Smell Container

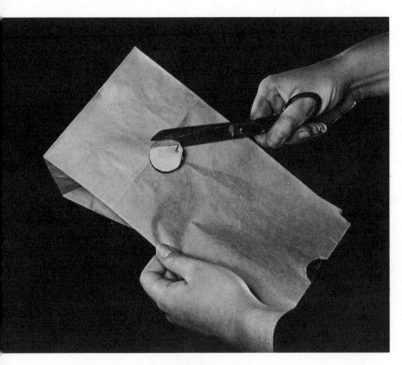

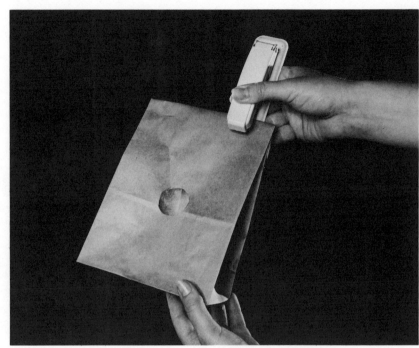

1. Cut a 1" hole in the middle of one side of the paper bag.

2. Put the object to be smelled inside the bag. Fold and staple the top of the bag shut.

You will need: *Paper bag, lunch bag size*
Plastic food storage bag
Scissors
Stapler

3. Have the child hold the paper bag with the hole to his nose and identify the object inside by the smell.

4. As a variation, line a paper bag with a plastic food storage bag. Place the smelly object inside the plastic bag. Twist the tops shut. Have the child untwist the bag slightly to smell and identify the object inside. The plastic bag prevents moisture from leaking through and tearing the bag.

Ice Cream Carton
Smell Container

1. Cut a hole in the middle of the lid of the ice cream container. Make the hole large enough for a child's nose to fit through.

You will need: *1 ice cream container*
Scissors

2. Place the object to be smelled in the
   container; secure the lid. Make sure
   the child cannot see the object he is
   trying to identify.

Shoe Box Smell Container

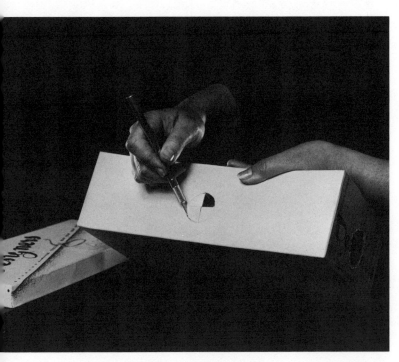

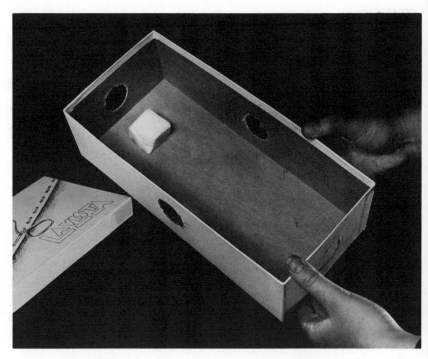

1. Cut a hole in the middle of each side of the shoe box. A child's nose should be able to fit inside the hole to smell an object.

2. Secure a smelly object to the inside of the box near one hole.

You will need: Shoe box
Scissors or X-acto knife
Tape

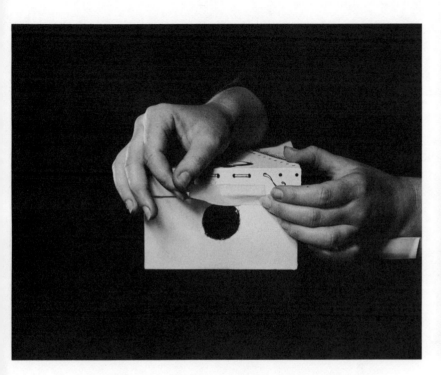

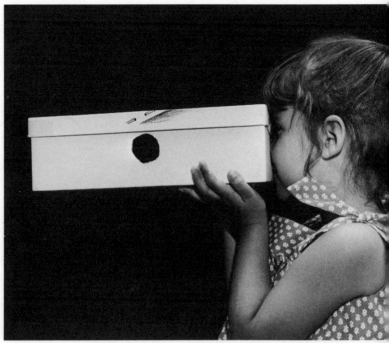

3. Secure the lid on the box with tape.

4. Have the child smell into each hole until he guesses what the object is and which hole gives off the strongest smell.

Sniff Bottles

1. If using the film containers, make several holes in each lid with the hammer and a nail. Place one type of item in each container and replace the lid.

2. If using the baby food jars, wrap one type of item in a piece of gauze and secure the lid. The child must remove the lid to smell what is inside. Make sure the child cannot see the object inside.

You will need: Hammer
Nail
Gauze
Plastic film containers or
baby food jars

Strong-smelling items to go into containers: peppercorns, cinnamon, cloves, onion flakes, lemon pepper, peanuts, cotton saturated with cooking extracts, oregano, cocoa, tea, etc.

3. The child smells each container and identifies it.

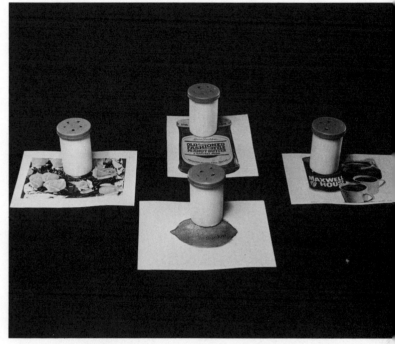

4. A picture of each item backed with cardboard and covered with clear contact paper can be used in identifying the smells.

Paper Bag Blindfold

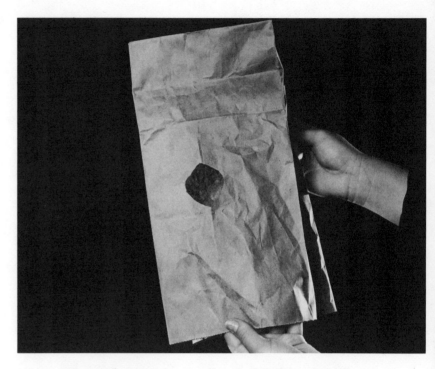

1. Place the bag over the child's head and mark the location of his nose on the bag. Remove the bag and cut a hole from the marked area.

You will need: *1   No. 12 paper bag*
                               Scissors

2. Place the bag over the child's head and
the blindfold is ready to use for smell
walks or smelling games.

Sunglass Blindfold

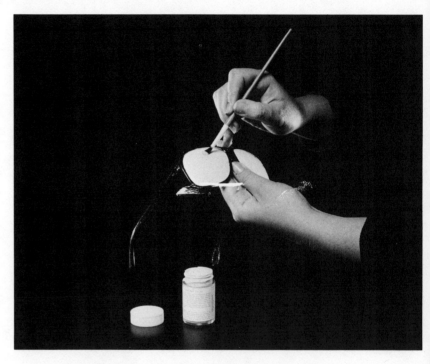

1. Paint the glasses with the gesso to block all vision from the glasses.

You will need: 1 *pair of wraparound sunglasses*
Gesso (purchased at art supply store)
or white paint
Paintbrush

2. When the gesso is dry, the sunglass blindfold is ready to use.

Halloween Mask Blindfold

1. Place masking tape over the eye holes on each side of the mask.

You will need: Halloween mask
Masking tape

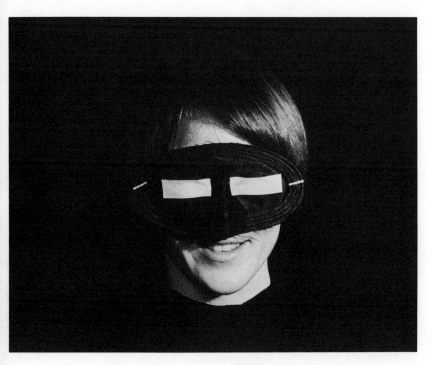

2. Use this mask to keep the child from
   seeing the objects he is trying to identify.

What's in the Bag?

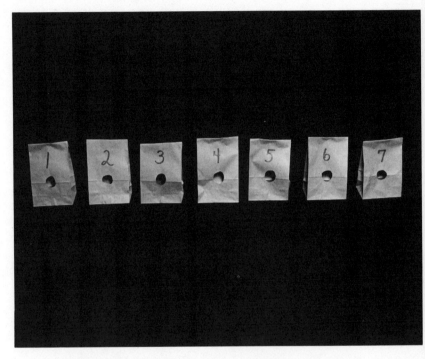

1. Make 7 plastic-lined paper bag smell containers. Fill each container with one object from the list of suggestions. (Bruising or opening the fruits or vegetables used will produce a stronger odor.) Number the bags from one to seven.

You will need: 7 paper sandwich bags
7 plastic food storage bags
Marking pen

Seven items from this list: onions, bell peppers, garlic, lemon, orange, parsley, mint, peanut butter, hard-boiled eggs, Brussels sprouts, Mentholatum, etc.

2. Have each child number his paper from one to seven. Have him smell each container and on his paper next to the corresponding number write what he thinks is in the container. If the child cannot write, he can verbalize his answers.

Smell Turntable

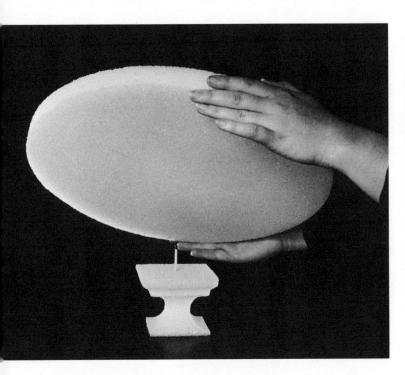

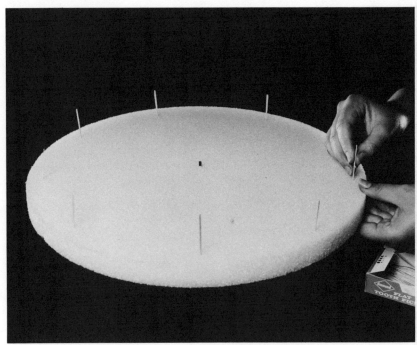

1. Connect the center of the circle to the middle of the base with dowel.

2. Stick toothpicks around the edges of the turntable.

You will need: 1 16″ diameter styrofoam circle
1 4″ styrofoam base
1 4″ x ⅛″ dowel
Toothpicks

Several of the following: orange rind, lemon rind; pieces of onion, bell pepper, carrot, cheese, pineapple, apple, chocolate, pickle; flower, olive, cinnamon stick, candies, peanuts, etc.

3. Secure one item on each tooth pick from the list above.

4. Blindfold the child. Spin the turntable to each item in turn and have the child smell and identify them.

Smell Cards

1. Cut several squares from the blotter paper. Use the cotton swab to spread the extract over one side of the blotter paper.

You will need: Blotter paper
Assortment of extracts
Cotton swabs
Marking pen

2. When the squares are dry, they are ready to be smelled and identified.

Smell Pads

1. Fold the 5″ x 8″ card in half to measure 5″ x 4″.

2. Cut a 2″ square of felt and glue this on the inside of the card.

You will need: 1 5″ x 8″ card   Glue
                    Felt   Extract
                    Scissors   Eye dropper

3. Have the child use the eye dropper to get a few drops of extract and squeeze it on the piece of felt.

4. Now smell the pad and identify the smell. The child may draw a picture of what he smells or choose a corresponding sticker to glue to his card.

Tired of Smelling

Have the child walk into a room where an odor is very prominent. Have him stand still for a few minutes and the odor will seem to lessen or disappear. The olfactory cells can lose their sensitivity to an odor after awhile.

You will need: One of the following—onions, room re-freshener, perfumes; foods that are cooking such as stew, spaghetti, cabbage, fish, etc.

Sniff Walk

Lay objects on one side of table with similar objects together. Blindfold child and have him begin smelling each object from one end of table to other. As soon as he smells a different odor, he says, "Change." Continue down table reporting odor changes. A game may be played by scoring one point for every smell change detected.

You will need:

1 long table
Blindfold

3 each of the following: lemons, oranges, eucalyptus leaves, soap, bell peppers, onions, smell pads with extracts, peanuts, coffee, flowers, grapefruits, tangerines, incense, etc.

Nature Smell Walk

1. Blindfold one child and have another child guide him on a smelling walk. Have the blindfolded child guess what he is smelling.

2. Flowers, leaves, bark, fruit trees, pine trees, dirt, animals, trash cans, cement, and fences are all good items to have the child smell. See pp. 92–102 for more smelling ideas.

You will need: *Blindfold*

3. Discovery walks may also be taken. Walk inside bakeries, doctor's offices, post offices, delicatessens, restaurants, and friends' homes to discover new smells. See pp. 99–101 for more ideas.

Diffusion

Open the bottle of extract and place it in a closed room. Leave the room for thirty minutes; then open the door and notice that the smell has spread through the room.

You will need: 1 bottle of peppermint extract

Perfumed Stationery

Holding the perfume bottle about 6″ away, spray each sheet of paper in the box and wave in the air to dry. When a letter is being written, the odor will be apparent, just as it will when the friend receives the letter.

You will need: 1 spray bottle of cologne or perfume
                            1 box of stationery

Flower and Herb Nosegays

1. Tie the flowers and herbs tightly together into a small bunch with some string or wire.

2. Cut the doilie from one edge to the midpoint.

You will need: *Fresh herbs and flowers: Mint, basil, sage, borage, bee balm, calendula, geranium leaves, lavender, rosemary, roses, sweet peas, etc.*

White paper doilie
String or floral wire
Ribbon

3. Wrap the doilie around the base of the nosegay. Staple or glue the cut edges together and tie a ribbon around the nosegay. It is ready to give to a friend in the hospital, as a May Day present, as a Mother's Day present, or for any special gift.

4. Certain flowers and herbs carry special meanings: rosemary, "Please remember me"; heather, "I admire you"; Forget-me-not, "I love you"; sage denotes esteem; borage cheers the heart.

Pomander Balls

1. Poke holes in the apple, orange, lime and lemon with the needle. Do not make the holes in a straight line as the skin might crack.

2. Put one whole clove in each hole.

You will need: 1 *box of whole cloves*
One or all of these: orange,
lemon, lime, apple
(should be firm and
fresh)

Cinnamon
Allspice
Nutmeg
Ground cloves

Large needle
Cheesecloth or
handkerchief
Nylon net
Ribbon

3. Place each fruit in a piece of cheese-cloth or handkerchief. Sprinkle the apple with cinnamon, orange with all-spice, lemon with ground cloves, and lime with nutmeg. Tie the cloth around the fruit and hang for three weeks.

4. After three weeks, shake off the excess spice and wrap each piece of fruit in a nylon net. Tie the net with a ribbon and hang the pomander balls in a room. Though the citrus fruits may shrink, they will keep their scent.

49

Perfume

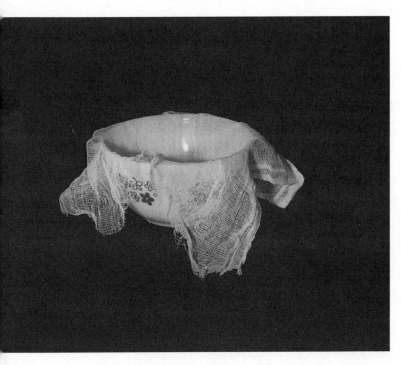

1. Line the inside of a bowl with cheese-cloth so edges overhang.

2. Tear enough flower petals into small pieces to measure one cup. Place in the cloth.

You will need: 1 cup fragrant flowers (roses, carnations, violets, lilac, lavender, orange blossoms, etc.)   1 cup water   Bowl   Cheesecloth or other soft cloth   Saucepan   Potholders   Funnel   Tiny jar with lid

3. Boil one cup of water and pour over petals until they are covered. Let soak overnight. The next day gather the corners of the cloth together and wring out all liquid. Discard petals. Put the scented water into a saucepan and boil until there is one tablespoon left.

4. Using a funnel, pour the perfume into a bottle and secure the lid. This perfume will last a month. A new fragrance can be created by using a new blend of flowers.

Incense Paper Cones

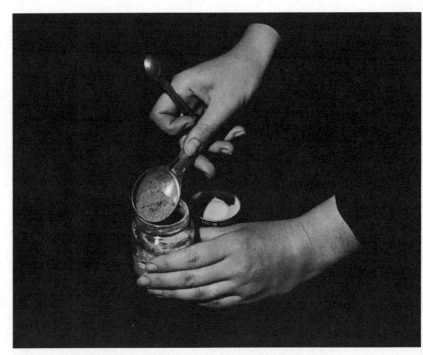

1. Sift the sawdust through a flour sifter until it is fine enough to burn.

2. Mix two tablespoons of powdered thyme with two tablespoons of sawdust in a jar and store until needed. Make another mixture by mixing two tablespoons sawdust, two tablespoons ginger and one tablespoon nutmeg together in a jar.

You will need:

1 large paper cone cup
1 jumbo paper clip
1 cup sawdust
2 tablespoons powdered thyme
2 tablespoons powdered ginger
1 tablespoon nutmeg
Flour sifter
Jar

3. Bend the jumbo paper clip into an S-shape holder with a base. Stand this holder in a bowl containing the thyme and sawdust mixture.

4. Cut off bottom inch of cone cup. Fill this small cone with incense mixture, place on paper clip holder, and ignite bottom end. A fragrance will fill the room. Keep the burning cone away from anything flammable. **Caution:** adult supervision absolutely essential for this activity.

Flower Potpourri

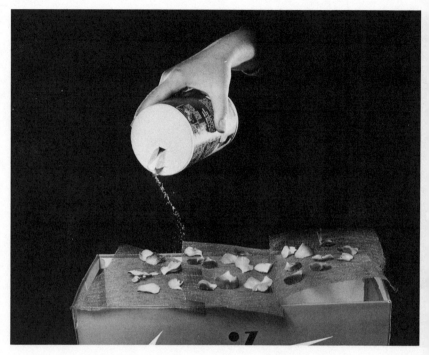

1. Remove the petals from the flower and add to the other materials and spices to be used. Put the screen over an open gift box or shoe box. Place the scented materials on the screen so the air can circulate around the petals.

2. Sprinkle uniodized salt over the petals and place in a dry, dark place.

You will need: Screen
Gift box or shoe box
Uniodized salt
Glass jar with tight-fitting lid
Orris or calamus root (buy at drugstore)

See next page for continuation of list

3. In a few days, the petals will be dry. Crush them and place them in a glass jar. Experiment with different combinations of flower petals, spices, and herbs to create special blends. For a richer scent, add ¾ teaspoon of orris or calamus root for every three cups of petals.

4. As a variation, making sachets is easy. Just follow directions for potpourri, except sprinkle spices such as cloves, cinnamon, or allspice over the dry petals. Wrap in a piece of sheer material and tie with a ribbon. Use to scent drawers and closets.

55

Flowers in full bloom and very dry: roses, carnations, honeysuckle, orange blossoms, lavender lilies, crab apple blossoms, delphinium, larkspur, lilacs, pansies, marigolds, and violas

Fragrant materials: mint, orange leaves, rose, rose geranium leaves, white oak bark, basis, calamus, lemon balm, lemon thyme, marjoram, patchouli, sweet lemongrass, sandalwood bark

Spices and miscellaneous: anise, allspice, caraway seeds, coriander seeds, mace, nutmeg, vanilla bean, cloves, cinnamon sticks, crushed and dried peel of lemon, lime, orange, and grapefruit

Recipes for Great Smells

Popcorn Fireworks

Spread the sheet on the floor. Place the popcorn popper in the middle of the sheet. Have the children sit around the edges of the sheet, far enough so hot popcorn will not hit them. Plug in the popper and add the popcorn. When the popcorn is hot enough, it will give a great "fireworks" display and a great smell. Quickly put the popcorn in a bag and add butter and salt. Shake and the popcorn is ready to serve. Adult supervision advised.

Baked Apples

You will need:

Apple corer
Paring knife
Saucepan
Stirring spoon
10" x 6" x 1½" baking dish

Recipe:

6 large baking apples
¾ cup raisins or chopped dates
1 cup brown sugar
1 cup water
2 tablespoons butter
½ teaspoon nutmeg

Preheat the oven to 350°. Have the children wash and core the apples. Pare a strip from the top of each baking apple. Fill each apple with the raisins or dates.

Combine the brown sugar, water, butter and spices in a saucepan and bring to a boil. Pour the hot syrup over and around the apples. Bake for 60 minutes, basting occasionally. Serve warm with cream. Don't forget to smell the room as the apples cook.

Applesauce

1. Have the children peel, core, and slice the apples into small pieces. Place the apples, water, and brown sugar into a bowl and mix. Sprinkle with cinnamon to taste.

2. Pour the ingredients into a hot frying pan. Have the children take turns stirring the apples until they are soft. This should take about 15 minutes.

You will need: Knife or peeler   10   Pippin apples
Bowl   2½   cups water
Stirring spoon   ¾   cup brown sugar
Frying pan   Cinnamon

3. Enjoy the smell of the room as the applesauce cooks. Have the children mash any whole pieces of apple that are left. After the applesauce has had time to cook, it will be ready to eat.

Crescent Cinnamon Rolls

You will need:

Saucepan
Shallow pan
Muffin tin

Recipe:

1 package of crescent rolls (Pillsbury or store brand, from dairy case)
½ cup butter
Large marshmallows
Cinnamon and sugar mixture

Melt the butter in a saucepan. Place cinnamon-sugar mixture in a shallow pan. Dip marshmallows in melted butter and then roll them in cinnamon-sugar mixture. Place the sugar-coated marshmallow in the center of a crescent roll and pinch the edges closed. Dip the roll in melted butter. Place in a muffin tin and bake as directed on the back of the can. The rolls will be hard to wait for once their aroma fills the kitchen.

Banana Nut Bread

You will need:

Mixing bowl and spoon, or electric mixer
Flour sifter
Measuring cup and spoons
9" x 5" x 3" loaf pan

Recipe:

⅓ cup shortening
½ cup sugar
2 eggs
1¾ cup unbleached flour
1 teaspoon baking soda
½ teaspoon salt
1 cup mashed ripe banana
½ cup chopped nuts

Preheat the oven to 350°. Have the children cream together the shortening and sugar, then add the eggs and beat well. Sift the dry ingredients together and add to the creamed mixture alternately with the banana. Be sure to blend well before adding each portion. Stir in the nuts. Pour into a greased and floured loaf pan. Bake 45 to 50 minutes or until done. Enjoy the smell that fills the room as the banana bread bakes. Remove from the pan and cool on a rack before serving.

Egg and Bacon Casserole

You will need:

Large skillet
Fork
Bowl
Eggbeater or mixing spoon

Recipe:

6 slices bacon
½ cup small croutons
6 eggs
⅓ cup milk
   Salt
   Pepper

Cook the bacon until crispy. Notice how the smell of bacon fills the room. Drain the bacon and have the children crumble it into coarse pieces. Save the bacon drippings. Place 1 tablespoon of drippings into a skillet, add the croutons and stir until brown and crisp. Remove from the skillet.

Add another tablespoon of drippings to the skillet. Combine eggs, milk, ½ teaspoon salt, and a dash of pepper; beat slightly. Pour into the skillet. Cook and stir until almost set; then add the bacon and croutons and cook until set. Serves 6.

Chili

You will need:

Large skillet with lid
Knife
Spoon

Recipe:

1 lb. ground beef
¾ cup chopped green pepper
1 cup chopped onion
1 1-lb. can of tomatoes
1 1-lb. can of kidney beans, drained
1 8-oz. can tomato sauce
1 teaspoon salt
1 teaspoon chili powder
1 bay leaf

In the skillet brown the meat, pepper, and onion. (Don't forget to enjoy the aroma.) Add the remaining ingredients; cover and simmer for one hour. As the chili cooks, notice how the smell fills the air. Remove the bay leaf and serve.

Spaghetti Sauce

You will need:

Large skillet or saucepan
Stirring spoon

Recipe:

1 onion
2 sticks of celery, chopped
4 tablespoons salad oil
3 6-oz. cans of tomato paste
1 24-oz. can of tomato puree
1 cup sliced mushrooms
1/8 cup parsley
3/4 teaspoon oregano
1 bay leaf
1 teaspoon salt
1/4 teaspoon pepper
1 1/2 pounds of ground meat

Cook the onion and celery in hot oil until tender and smell the odor that fills the room. Add the meat and cook until browned. Add remaining ingredients and simmer uncovered 2–2½ hours. A new odor will fill the air. Remove the bay leaf and serve over cooked spaghetti.

Cooking Spaghetti

You will need:

Extra large kettle
Fork or spaghetti lifter
Colander

Recipe:

12-oz. package spaghetti
3–4 quarts water
1 tablespoon salt

Bring water to a rapid boil. Gradually drop spaghetti into water. Stir with fork to separate spaghetti. Cook uncovered at a fast boil, stirring occasionally to prevent sticking. Test the spaghetti after 4–5 minutes by checking one piece. It should be tender to the bite but still firm. When done, remove from kettle with fork or lifter and let drain in a colander. Serve immediately.

Stew

You will need:

Knife
Large pot with lid
Stirring spoon

Recipe:

1 lb. stew meat, boiled or sautéed ahead
   of time
1 teaspoon salt
1 can condensed tomato soup
1 can water
3 carrots
3 potatoes
3 onions

Have the children slice the carrots, potatoes and onions. Put all the ingredients in a pot. Simmer until the vegetables and meat are tender, about 1½ hours. As the stew cooks, its odor will fill the air. If there is not enough juice, add water; if the stew is too thin, take off the lid and cook the sauce until thickened.

Fish in a Blanket

You will need:

Electric frying pan
Pastry brush
Large spatula or pancake turner
Spreading knife

Recipe:

¼ cup melted butter or margarine
2 tablespoons lemon juice
1 8-oz. package of frozen breaded fish
   sticks
5 frankfurter buns
Tartare sauce or sandwich spread

Combine the melted butter and lemon juice. Have the children dip the fish sticks into the mixture and place in an electric frying pan. Brush the fish sticks with lemon butter and turn once. Follow directions on the back of the package for temperature and length of cooking. Toast the buns while smelling the odor of fish cooking in the room. Spread the buns with tartare sauce or sandwich spread; place two fish sticks in each and serve.

Tasting Experiences

Tasting and Smelling

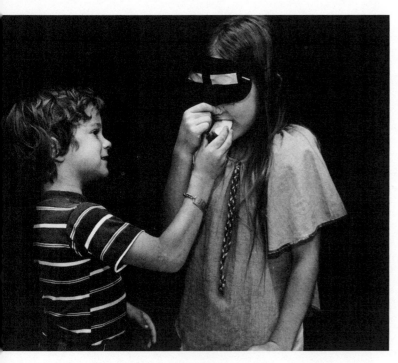

1. Place a blindfold on one child and have him close his nose with his fingers. Give him one selection of food or juice to eat or drink.

2. Let the child guess what he is tasting. If the child cannot guess, let him open his nose and attempt to name the type of food once more. This experiment shows that the two senses of taste and smell work together so closely that part of what is called taste is often smell.

You will need: One each of the following: potato, celery, apple, carrot, onions, turnip, bell pepper, etc.
One each of the following: grape juice, tomato juice, orange juice, lemonade, apple juice, etc.
Blindfold

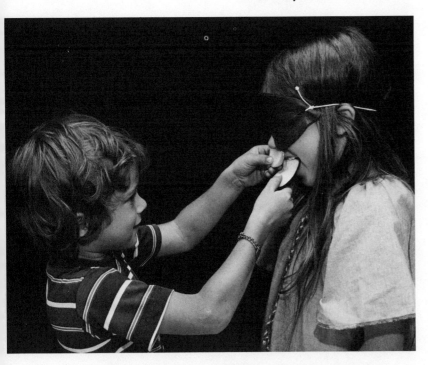

3. As a variation, blindfold one child and hold a piece of onion to his nose while he tastes a piece of apple. The child will probably guess he is eating an onion.

Dry Tongue Cannot Taste

1. Dry a child's tongue with a handkerchief.

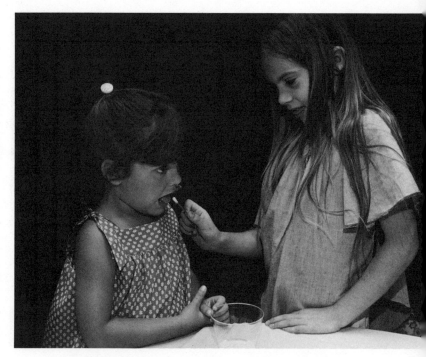

2. Put a few granules of sugar on the tip of the child's tongue. As long as the tongue remains dry the child will not be able to taste the sweetness.

3. Have the child close his mouth. This will cause the saliva to dissolve the sugar so it can be tasted.

Taste Bud Areas

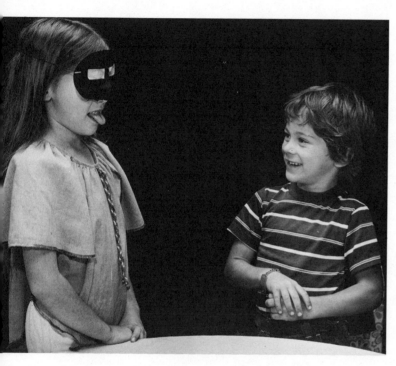

1. Have the child stick out his tongue. Make sure he cannot see the materials used for this experiment. Dip a toothpick into water and then into some sugar. Apply this to the tip of the child's tongue. The child should recognize a sweet taste.

2. Have child take a drink of water and stick his tongue out again. Dip toothpick into water and sugar and place it on front right side of child's tongue. He may not be quite sure of the taste. Repeat this test further back on right side, on middle back of tongue, and on two spots on left side. Be sure the child takes a drink of water between each test.

You will need: 2 glasses of water   Vinegar   Honey
Sugar   Instant coffee gran-   Jello
Salt   ules   Dill pickle juice
Quinine water   Lemon juice   Toothpicks or cotton
Bitter chocolate   swabs

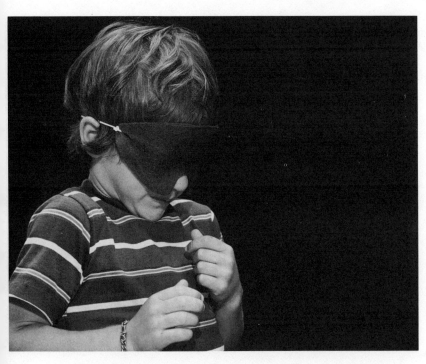

3. Repeat with all or some of materials from list above and child will begin to notice that certain parts of his tongue taste certain things. The four tastes of sweet, sour, bitter, and salty are the only tastes that do not require smell. Taste bud areas of the tongue are: sweet, tip of tongue; salty, front sides of tongue; sour, back sides of tongue behind salty area; bitter, middle back of tongue.

Distinguishing Foods
Which Look Alike

1. This tasting experience will allow children to discover that foods that look alike do not always taste the same.

2. Have the child taste some of the pairs of food and identify the food. Children soon realize that a piece of potato may look like a piece of apple, but the differences in taste are quite different.

You will need: Pairs of the following foods—
Powdered sugar   /   flour
Granulated sugar   /   salt
Cantaloupe   /   sweet potato
White potato   /   apple
Bread   /   pound cake
Carrot   /   sweet potato
Pumpkin   /   sweet potato
Turnip   /   white potato
Cucumber   /   apple

Tired of Tasting

1. Have the child add sugar to his tea to his desire and take a few sips.

2. Have the child eat a teaspoon of jam.

You will need: 1 *teaspoon jam*
Cup of hot tea
Sugar
Spoon

3. Have the child take another drink of tea. Does it taste sweet enough? Usually the tea doesn't seem as sweet. Nothing has happened to the sugar, but the taste cells have been so stimulated by the very sweet jam that they cannot sense ordinary sweetness of the sugar in the tea.

Tongue Sensitivity

Have the child taste an assortment of foods and drinks. Have him describe their textures and temperatures.

You will need: *Foods that are smooth:*

> *Pudding, ice cream, cream cheese, cheese, sour cream, yogurt, popsicles, etc.*

Foods that are rough:

> *Tapioca pudding, rice, cereal, cottage cheese, bread, crackers, etc.*

Foods or drinks that are cold:

> *Milk, soda, juices, ice cream, ice, popsicles, raw vegetables, fruits, cheese, etc.*

Foods or drinks that are hot:

> *Potatoes, hot chocolate, tea, soup, hot cereal, cooked meat and vegetables, hot cider, etc.*

Taste Connoisseur

This experiment will show how the sense of taste can be developed so well that a person can differentiate between different blends of teas. Have the child taste various blends of teas and describe each one noting differences. This experiment could be done with cheese, Jello, Kool-aid, soup broths, coffees and sodas.

You will need: Hot water
Tea cups
Variety of teas: Orange Pekoe, Earl Grey, China Black,
Celon Breakfast tea, herb teas, Red Zinger tea, Constant
Comment tea, etc.

Strawberry Stickum

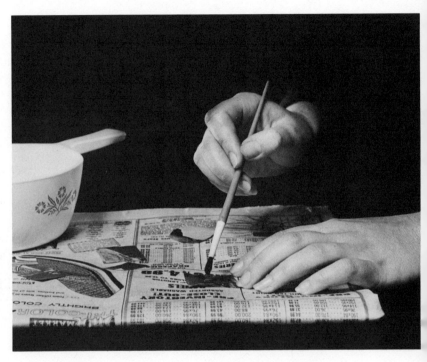

1. Cut out colored pictures from a slick magazine and lay them face down on newspaper.

2. Place the water and gelatin into a saucepan, bring to a boil over medium heat, and stir constantly until the gelatin dissolves. Remove from the heat and let cool for a minute. With the stickum still warm, paint an even coat on the back of each picture with a new paintbrush.

You will need:
1 tablespoon strawberry gelatin
2 teaspoons water
Slick magazine

Scissors
Newspaper
Paintbrush

3. Let the stamps dry for two days. They will curl as they dry. Enjoy the taste as you lick them and stick them to envelopes, stationery, notebooks, or anything else they will adhere to.

Taste and Smell Sources

Taste Sources

Salty

Crackers
Pretzels
Chips
Peanuts
Nuts
Salty bagels
Corned beef
Bacon
Bouillon

Sweet

Sugar
Honey
Gelatin desserts
Whipped cream
Fresh ripe fruit
Sweetened powdered drink mixes
Molasses
Jams and jellies
Pancake syrup

Note: These lists of taste sources are by no means complete. Add to them as many others as you wish.

Sour

Sour cream
Vinegar
Buttermilk
Mustard
Pomegranates
Lemons
Limes
Pickles
Plain yogurt
Grapefruit

Bitter

Horseradish
Radishes
Purple onions
Cocoa
Unsweetened chocolate

Household Smell Sources

Fresh vegetables

Potatoes
Tomatoes
Carrots
Lettuce
Celery
Beets
Parsley
Spinach
Zucchini
Broccoli
Cauliflower
Green beans
Sweet corn
Peas
Radishes
Brussels sprouts
Cabbage
Mushrooms
Bean sprouts
Yellow squash
Sweet potatoes
Onions
Green peppers
Pumpkin

Fresh fruits

Lemons
Limes
Oranges
Apples
Grapefruit
Peaches
Canteloupes
Tangerines
Apricots
Plums
Bananas
Strawberries
Pomegranates
Cherries
Grapes
Nectarines
Watermelon
Pineapples
Mangoes
Papayas
Avocados

Canned and packaged foods

Onion juice
Garlic juice
Parsley flakes
Chicken bouillon
Beef bouillon
Imitation bacon bits
Tea
Coffee
Soy sauce
Vinegar
Peanuts
Sugar
Cocoa
Molasses
Jams
Jellies
Gelatin desserts
Syrups
Hot sauce
Mustard
Crackers
Cereals

Cheese
Tuna
Sardines
Pickles
Cookies
Meats
Eggs
Soups
Honey
Whipping cream
Powdered drink mixes
    (sweetened and unsweetened)
Canned fruit drinks
Pretzels
Chips
Nuts
Salty bagels
Corned beef
Sour cream
Vinegar
Buttermilk
Horseradish

Household Smell Sources

Soaps

Dishwashing soap
Laundry soap
Liquid detergent
Bathroom hand soaps
Cleansers
Spray cleaners

Packaged personal care products

Hand creams
Lotions
Shampoos
Toothpastes
Perfumes
Cold and pain rubs (Vicks Vapo-Rub,
    Mentholatum, Ben-Gay, etc.)

Oils

Lemon
Bergamot
Lavender
Peppermint
Verbena
Cinnamon
Bitter almond
Musk
Sage
Rosemary
Sweet orange
Sassafras
Soybean
Cottonseed
Caraway
Cassia
Coumarin
Jasmine
Gardenia
Clove
Rose
Sandalwood
Patchouli
Geranium
Coconut
Palm
Olive
Peanut

Extracts

Vanilla
Chocolate
Butterscotch
Peppermint
Lemon
Orange
Strawberry
Banana
Maple
Almond
Pineapple
Anise

Spices and herbs

Sage
Parsley
Thyme
Rosemary
Oregano
Mint
Basil
Bay leaves
Chili powder
Pepper
Lemon pepper
Dill
Paprika
Mace
Saffron
Caraway
Cinnamon
Nutmeg
Ginger
Allspice
Clove
Comino
Fennel
Marjoram

Miscellaneous

Incense
Scented candles
Room fresheners
Toys (rubber, plastic,
    and metal)
Paint
Clay
Moth balls

Backyard Smell Sources

Plants and Flowers

Ambrosian
Bee balm
Clove pink
Feverfew
Lemon verbena
Lemon balm
Lavender
Mint (peppermint, spearmint,
    lemon, and apple)
Lily-of-the-valley
Lavender cotton
Peony
Rosemary
Sweet marjoram
Sweet woodruff
Thyme
Tarragon
Tansy
Violet
Gardenia
Peppermint geranium
Scented leaf geranium
Sweet pea

Marigold
Pansy
Marguerite
Poppy
Viola
Tulip
Daffodil
Carnation
Iris
Stock
Phlox
Hollyhock
Petunia
Moss rose
Dandelion
Coleus
Begonia
Caladium
Gladiolus
Zinnia
Larkspur
Delphinium
Daisies

Trees and Shrubs
(smell the bark and leaves by slightly bruising them)

Maple
Oak
Elm
Spruce
Fir
Pine
Apple
Pear
Cherry
Peach
Orange
Lemon
Lime
Grapefruit
Lilac
Bridal wreath
Pussy willow
Dogwood
Mock orange

Miscellaneous

Dirt
Fences (metal, wood, brick)
Grass
Cement
Animals
Trash cans
Cars
Bikes
Garages

Community Smell Sources

Place	Smells to notice
Doctor's office	Medicine and disinfectants
Dentist's office	Medicine and disinfectants
Hospital	Medicine and disinfectants
Gas station	Gas, oil, dirt
Grocery store	Meats, fruits, vegetables, dairy products, etc.
Delicatessen	Meats, cheeses, spices, pizza
Bakery	Breads and pastries

Place	Smell to notice
Restaurants (Mexican, Italian, Chinese, etc.; seafood, steak, etc.)	Distinctive kinds of foods
Candy store	Chocolate, licorice, peanut brittle, etc.
Airport	Fuels, dust
Bus station	Gas fumes, dust
Park	Trees, flowers, grass
Florist	Variety of flowers
Body shop	Welding, paint
Dump	Rotten odors
Candle store	Variety of candle scents
Beach	Salt water, ocean breeze, barbecues
Mountains	Trees, clean air
Beauty and barber shops	Shampoos, hair spray, permanent wave solution, talcum powder, shaving cream
Laundromat	Clean and dirty clothes, soaps, hot moist air
Church	Wood, flowers, cleanliness
Dry cleaner	Steam presses, chemicals
Plant nursery	Fertilizer, plants, trees
Pet store	Animal odors
Gymnasium	Perspiration
Lumber yard	Fresh-cut wood
Hardware store	Metals
Department store	Changes from department to department

Place	**Smell to notice**
Print shop	Printing ink, machinery
Paint store	Paint, turpentine
Swimming pool	Chlorine
Fabric store	Cloth and lint
Movie theater	Popcorn and soft drinks

Fragrant Plants

Many weeds and plants can be ignited to enhance the enjoyment of their fragrant parts. We hope no one would destroy a tree or shrub just to burn it. Use parts which are already dead or spare parts left over after the plant has been put to some useful purpose. All of the plants listed here are pleasant to smell as they burn but also have identifiable smells as green plants.

Deer tongue or wild vanilla: An herb dried, tied in bunches, and burned. It has a mild vanilla scent that is good to use in potpourri mixes.

Rosemary: Use green or dry for a fragrant clean smell.

Spanish iris or orrisroot: Grows semi-wild through the south. The roots are dried and then burned for a fragrant odor. Used in perfumes, cosmetics and dental preparations.

Scotch pine: Many pine tree roots are fragrant but this one is specially delightful to smell.

Elecampane or elfwort: This weed grows along shaded roadsides and in slightly damp meadows. The flower is yellow and resembles rays of sun. The root resembles a toy wooden top. Cut the roots, dry them and burn for fragrance.

Lavender: Lavender grows in a slender spike from one to three feet tall. All of its parts are fragrant and even more so after it dries.

Sweet Recipes

Suicide Drink

1. Let each child pour a little of each juice into his cup to create his own concoction.

You will need: A variety of fruit juices: apple, boysenberry, grape, grapefruit, orange, pineapple; lemonade; strawberry nectar, peace nectar, apricot nectar, etc.

2. Have the children discuss what they put in their drink and how it tasted.

Tropical Delight

You will need:

  2 *cups orange juice*
  2 *cups lemon juice*
  2 *cups grenadine*
2½ *quarts ginger ale*

Mix all the ingredients together for a delicious sweet drink. (Serves 24.)

Additional Sweet Beverages

Floats

Put a scoop of ice cream, ice milk, or sherbet into each child's cup of punch or soda pop. Use large cups, and distribute spoons.

Flavored milk

Mix one of the following with milk: orange or grape-flavored Tang, or strawberry or chocolate Nestle's Quik.

Eggnog

Beat together 1 dozen eggs (2 dozen for richer eggnog) 1½ gallons of milk, 3 cups of honey, 2 tablespoons of vanilla flavoring. Pour into cups and sprinkle nutmeg on the top. Makes 36 servings.

Smoothies

Put 2 cups of fruit juice, ½ cup of powdered milk, ½ teaspoon vanilla, and 1 scoop of ice cream or ice milk into a quart jar. Screw the lid on tightly and shake until smooth. Each jar will serve 4 children.

Bubble juice

Follow the directions on a can of fruit juice concentrate, but use soda water instead of tap water to reconstitute the juice.

Hot cider

Add 2 cinnamon sticks to each gallon of cider; then heat and serve.

Hot chocolate

Make this a special drink by giving each child a candy peppermint stick with which to stir his hot chocolate, or drop miniature marshmallows into each cup.

Fruit Dips

You will need:

Apples
Oranges
Bananas
Pineapple
Grapes
Strawberries
Sour cream
Brown sugar
Marshmallow cream
Chocolate sauce
Coconut
Chopped nuts
Powdered sugar and cocoa mixture
Cinnamon and sugar mixture

Slice or cut up the various pieces of fruit and let the children experiment with the different condiments. Observe how the taste of the fruit may change.

Fruit Kabob

You will need:

Large bowl
Spoon
Skewers

Recipe:

3 peaches, skinned and cut in half
3 bananas, sliced thick
2 apples, sliced in wedges
1 fresh pineapple, cubed
3 grapefruits, sectioned
1 cup grapefruit juice
½ cup honey
1 teaspoon chopped mint

Mix the grapefruit juice, honey, and mint together. Marinate the fruit in this mixture for 30 minutes; then place on skewers, alternating fruits. Broil for 5 minutes, basting frequently with the marinade.

Yogurt Popsicles

You will need:

    Large pitcher
    Long-handled spoon
16 3-oz. paper cups
16 Popsicle sticks

Recipe:

1   quart plain yogurt
1   12-oz. can concentrated unsweetened
        fruit juice (orange juice works
        well)
¼   cup honey
1   tablespoon vanilla extract

Mix the ingredients together in a large pitcher. Pour into 3-oz. paper cups and freeze. Insert a popsicle stick in the middle of the cup when the mixture is partially frozen.

Strawberry Mousse

You will need:

Large measuring cup
Small, deep mixing bowl
Large mixing bowl
Greased gelatin mold

Recipe:

1 16-oz. package frozen sliced
     strawberries
1 envelope unflavored gelatin
1 cup boiling water
1 cup heavy cream
½ cup sugar
1 teaspoon vanilla

Defrost and drain strawberries. Pour juice into large measuring cup and add enough water to make 1 cup liquid. Pour in gelatin; stir and let soften 5 minutes. Add 1 cup boiling water and stir until gelatin is dissolved. Add strawberries and cool for 30 minutes or until slightly thickened. In another bowl, beat cream until frothy; gradually add sugar and vanilla. Transfer strawberry gelatin mixture into large bowl. Fold in whipped cream. Pour mousse into greased mold and chill for 3 hours.

Peanut Butter Goodies

You will need:

Large mixing bowl
Mixing spoon
Measuring cup and spoons
Storage container

Recipe:

½ cup peanut butter
½ cup honey
½ cup instant cocoa or carob protein
      powder
 1 cup toasted wheat germ
 1 cup peanuts or soy nuts
½ cup sunflower seeds
    Coconut

Combine all the ingredients except for the coconut. Roll the mixture into walnut-size balls. Roll in coconut and store in the refrigerator until ready to eat.

Chocolate Cookie Roll

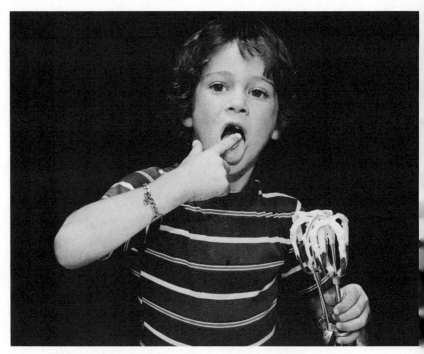

1. Whip the cream until frothy; then add the vanilla and sugar. Continue beating until thick.

2. Spread one side of each cookie with whipped cream and arrange the cookies on a plate to make a long roll. Frost the cookie roll with the remainder of whipped cream.

You will need: Narrow mixing bowl
Electric mixer
Knife or spatula
Serving plate
Measuring cup and spoons

Recipe: 12 thin chocolate cookies
1 cup heavy cream
½ teaspoon vanilla extract
1 teaspoon sugar

3. Chill in the refrigerator for 4 hours.

4. Slice the roll at an angle so the pieces have stripes of cream and chocolate cookie. Enjoy this sweet treat.

Additional Sweet Snacks

Frosted goodies

Provide frosting that has been prepared ahead of time or let the children make their own. Different flavors and colors make the experience more interesting. Let the children do one of the following: (1) put frosting between 2 vanilla wafers; (2) put frosting between 2 graham crackers; (3) frost plain cookies; (4) frost plain cupcakes or donuts. (Honey-butter can be used instead of frosting. Make it by mixing ½ cup honey with a ¼-lb. stick of soft butter until smooth.)

Homemade ice cream or sherbet

Children love taking turns turning the crank of a manual freezer. Use a recipe from any cookbook.

Frozen Dixie bars

The children should prepare this recipe one week ahead of time. Pour Kool-aid or fruit juice into small paper cups. From some poster-board, cut a circle slightly larger than mouth of cup; insert Popsicle stick through slit in center of circle. Put stick into liquid and let lid rest on top of cup. Place in freezer and freeze solid. At serving time, the children can peel off the paper cups and eat. For variety, drop small pieces of fruit into juice before freezing.

Ice cream cones

Sherbet, ice cream, or ice milk can be used.

Cookies

Fresh, hot cookies right out of the oven are always a favorite. Use any simple cookie recipe or a boxed cookie mix. Rolling cookies, cutting them with cookie cutters, baking them and decorating them is a valid craft project as well as a cooking experience.

No-melt finger Jello

The children should prepare this recipe one week ahead of time. Mix four packages of unflavored gelatin, one cup cold water, 3 small packages of Jello (any flavor) and ½ cup sugar in a 9″ x 13½″ x 2″ pan. Add 4 cups boiling water, stir until gelatin and Jello are dissolved. Refrigerate until firm; then cut into 1″ cubes. Roll cubes lightly in powdered sugar.

Cone cup cake

Prepare batter for package cake (use directions on box) and pour batter into flat-bottomed ice cream cones until they are about half full. Bake at 350° for 1 hour or until lightly browned. Each cone can be frosted and decorated if desired.

Pudding

Prepare any kind of boxed pudding according to directions on box. Serve pudding in small paper cups (warm or cool). Vanilla, chocolate, custard, and tapioca are always favorites.

Cocoa bananas

Cut 12 bananas into fourths. Roll each section in mixture of 1 cup confectioner's sugar and 4 tablespoons cocoa. (This mixture is also a good coating for other kinds of fruits.) Sprinkle with chopped nuts and top with whipped cream.

Peanut butter globs

Mix together 1 cup peanut butter, 1 cup corn syrup, 1½ cups powdered nonfat milk, and 1¼ cups sifted powdered sugar. Roll mixture into balls. For variety, put 2 or 3 peanuts into center of each ball.

Rice Krispie treats

Follow recipe on Rice Krispie box. For variety, use 2 packages of crisp Chinese noodles instead of Rice Krispies, or add *one* of the following to standard recipe: ¼ cup peanut butter, peanuts, coconut, raisins, chocolate chips, butterscotch chips, etc.

Special-K treats

Mix 1 cup corn syrup, 1 cup sugar, and 1½ cups peanut butter in pan. Heat and stir until smooth. Add 4 cups Special-K cereal and mix thoroughly. Drop from teaspoon onto greased cookie sheet or waxed paper. Cool and eat.

S' Mores

Separate graham crackers into squares and place on cookie sheet. Put half a plain Hershey bar on each square and top with large marshmallow. Broil in oven until marshmallows are toasted. Put another graham cracker square on top and serve warm.

Chinese Snoodles

Melt together one large package of chocolate chips and one large package of butterscotch chips. Remove from heat and add one large can of Virginia peanuts and 12 oz. of crisp Chinese noodles. Mix thoroughly. Drop from a teaspoon onto a greased cookie sheet or waxed paper.

Biscuit cinnamon rolls

Provide several cans of refrigerator biscuits. Flatten each biscuit and spread it with soft butter or margarine. Sprinkle sugar and cinnamon on the butter and roll the biscuit into a roll. Place on greased cookie sheet and bake according to directions on can.

Apricot Coconut Candies

You will need:

Double boiler
Food grinder
Breadboard or other surface to knead on
Wax paper
Storage container

Recipe:

1 cup dried apricots
1 cup flaked coconut
¾ cup chopped nuts
1 teaspoon grated lemon rind
1 tablespoon lemon juice
1 tablespoon orange juice
   Confectioner's sugar

In top of double boiler, heat apricots over boiling water for 10 minutes. Put apricots, coconut, and nuts through food grinder, using fine blade. Knead mixture with lemon rind, lemon, and orange juice. Add enough confectioner's sugar to firm the mixture. Form into walnut-size balls, roll in confectioner's sugar, and dry at room temperature for 4 hours. A sweet treat.

Quick Coconut Pie

You will need:

Saucepan
Mixing bowl
Spoons

Recipe:

1 cup milk
3 tablespoons butter
3 eggs
½ cup sugar
½ cup light corn syrup
½ teaspoon vanilla extract
½ teaspoon coconut extract
1 cup shredded coconut
1 prepared, unbaked pie shell

Heat milk and butter together in saucepan over very low heat until butter is melted. In mixing bowl, beat eggs until foamy. Add sugar, light corn syrup, vanilla and coconut extracts. Combine milk and egg mixtures and mix well. Spread shredded coconut in pie shell; pour milk and egg mixture over coconut. Bake at 350° for 40 minutes or until set.

Sour Recipes

Nuts and Bolts

You will need:

Measuring cup
Large bowl

Recipe:

4 cups Rice Chex
4 cups Wheat Chex
4 cups pretzels
1 cup peanuts
½ cup butter or margarine
  Lawry's Seasoning Salt

Mix the cereals, pretzels, and peanuts together in a bowl. Melt the butter and season to taste with the Lawry's Seasoning Salt. Pour over the dry ingredients, toss lightly, and serve this salty treat.

Cheesy Peanut Spread

You will need:

Medium mixing bowl
Knife or spreader

Recipe:

1 8 oz. package of cream cheese, softened
1 package powdered French dressing
   Chopped salty peanuts
   Salty crackers

Combine the cream cheese and French dressing. Mix well and form into a large ball. Roll the cheese ball in the chopped peanuts. Serve on a salty cracker. You may need something to quench your thirst after you have had a few of these.

Salami and Cheese Rollups

You will need:

Salami slices
Cheese
Toothpicks

Have the child top a slice of salami with a slice of cheese and roll it up. The salami and cheese rolls are ready to eat for a salty treat. Try also the variations in the next column.

Tree trunks: Take one slice of bologna and one slice of cheese and roll together. Stick a toothpick through the roll.

Ham and cheese squares: Put one slice of ham on top of one slice of cheese. Continue to stack the ham and cheese on top of each other until there are six layers. Cut the stack into little squares and put a toothpick through each square.

French Fries

You will need:

Deep fryer or deep saucepan
Deep-fry basket
Paper towel

Recipe:

1½ lbs. potatoes (4 medium)
    Salad oil or shortening
    Salt
    Ketchup

Cut the potatoes into lengthwise strips ¼″ wide. Fill a deep fryer or deep saucepan half full with salad oil and heat to 375°. Fill the basket a quarter full with potatoes and lower into the hot oil. Fry five to seven minutes or until the potatoes are golden. Remove from oil and drain on paper towels. Salt to taste. Repeat until all the potatoes are fried. Eat plain or with ketchup.

BLT Sandwich

You will need:

Skillet
Fork
Knife or other spreader

Recipe:

Bacon slices
Tomatoes
Lettuce
Mayonnaise
Choice of bread (toasted if desired)

Fry the bacon until crispy and drain. Spread mayonnaise on the bread; add a layer of cooked bacon slices, tomato slices, and lettuce. Top with another slice of bread. Bacon makes a salty tasting sandwich.

Tuna Fish Casserole

You will need:

Large mixing bowl
Measuring cup and spoons
Mixing spoon
1½-qt. casserole dish

Recipe:

1   7-oz. can tuna fish (drained)
1   can cream of mushroom soup
½   cup milk
½   teaspoon salt
1   cup crushed potato chips
    Margarine

Preheat oven to 375°. Grease the baking dish with margarine. Combine the cream of mushroom soup and milk in a bowl and stir until well blended. Break the tuna into chunks and place it in the bottom of the casserole. Pour the diluted cream of mushroom soup over the tuna and top with the crushed potato chips. Bake at 375° for 25 minutes.

Chipped Beef

You will need:

Saucepan
Mixing spoon

Recipe:

1 can cream of chicken soup
½ can of milk
1 large package chipped beef
Choice of bread, toasted

Combine the cream of chicken soup with the milk in a saucepan and heat. Add the chipped beaf and simmer for 5 minutes. Pour over a slice of toast. This will have a salty taste. Serves 4.

Corned Beef Hash

You will need:

Skillet with lid
Mixing bowl
Mixing spoon

Recipe:

1 cup canned corned beef hash
2 tablespoons ketchup
1 teaspoon dried onion flakes
4 tablespoons bacon fat

Combine the hash, catsup, and onion flakes, and sauté in bacon fat in a covered skillet. Cook 10 minutes over low heat; then serve. Ketchup may be added on top of the hash. Serves 4.

Teriyaki

You will need:

Mixing bowl
Mixing spoon
Baking dish
Shallow pan
Skewers
Barbecue grill

Soy Sauce Marinade:

1 cup soy sauce
¼ cup sugar
2 cloves garlic
2 teaspoons fresh grated ginger
1 teaspoon MSG

Combine all the ingredients together in a small bowl. Use for Teriyaki recipes.

Chicken Wings Teriyaki

2 lbs. chicken wings
1 cup soy sauce marinade

Preheat oven to 350°. Wash and dry the chicken wings. Place the chicken wings in a baking dish and cover with half the marinade. Bake for 45 minutes. Stir the wings and add the remainder of the marinade and bake for 25 minutes more.

Teriyaki Beef

Sirloin steak
Soy sauce marinade

Cut the meat into rectangles. Place three pieces on a skewer. Place in a shallow pan and cover with soy sauce marinade. Refrigerate for one or two hours. When the barbecue coals are hot, place the skewers of meat on the grill. Cook on one side for three to five minutes. Turn the skewers to the other side and grill until the meat is done to your liking.

Roasted Pumpkin Seeds

You will need:

Baking pan
Knife
Spoon

Recipe:

Pumpkin
Salt
Butter

Scrape out the insides of a pumpkin and save the seeds. Wash the seeds in a flat pan to rid them of any pumpkin membrane. Drain the seeds and spread them in a baking pan. Sprinkle salt over the seeds, and add a few teaspoons of butter. Roast in a 300° oven, stirring occasionally to brown the seeds evenly. They are finished when brown and crisp. Eat shells and all.

Salty Recipes

Lemonade

You will need:

Measuring cup
Long-handled stirring spoon
Large pitcher

Recipe:

3 cups water
1 cup lemon juice (4 lemons)
¼ cup sugar
Ice

Combine the lemon juice, water and sugar. Pour over the ice. This will be very sour. Add sugar to sweeten the lemonade to taste. Make five ¾-cup servings.

Hot Dog Sauce

You will need:

Small bowl
Spoon

Recipe:

2 tablespoons mustard
1 tablespoon relish

Combine the ingredients together and spread on a hot dog bun for a sour and tangy hot dog sauce. Serves 2.

Rhubarb Sauce

You will need:

Knife
Measuring cup
Saucepan with lid
Stirring spoon

Recipe:

3 cups rhubarb, cut into 1″ pieces
½–¾ cups sugar
¼ cup water

Combine all the ingredients together in a pot. Bring to a boil; cover and cook slowly until tender, about five minutes. Eat this sauce plain or on ice cream. The more sugar you add, the sweeter the taste.

Cranapple Relish

You will need:

Food grinder
Knife
Measuring spoon
Mixing spoon
Small bowl

Recipe:

12 cranberries
¼ unpeeled and cored apple
2 teaspoons sugar
   Orange peel from a small section
      of an orange
   Food grinder

Grind the cranberries, apple, and orange peel into a bowl. Add the sugar and mix well. Serve on poultry, toast, or in a sandwich.

Lemon Curd Tarts

Recipe:

Grated rind of 2 medium lemons
½ cup lemon juice
2 cups sugar
1 cup butter or margarine
4 eggs, well beaten
4 dozen miniature tart shells, sugar
    cookies, or shortbread cookies

1. Combine the lemon rind, juice and sugar in the top of a double boiler. Add the butter and heat over boiling water stirring constantly. Stir until the mixture is thick enough to mound, about 15 minutes.

You will need: *Grater*
Measuring cup
Double boiler
Mixing spoon

2. Cool thoroughly and spoon into tart shells or on top of the cookies. This will be a sour tasting experience.

Tossed Salad with Oil and Vinegar Dressing

You will need:

Colander
Measuring cup and spoons
Mixing spoon
Medium-sized jar with lid
Salad bowl

Recipe:

Lettuce
Tomatoes
Celery
Cucumbers
½ cup salad oil
2 tablespoons wine or cider vinegar
½ teaspoon salt
⅛ teaspoon pepper
1 clove garlic
1 tablespoon water

Wash the vegetables and prepare them for the salad. Combine the salt, pepper and garlic together and combine with the vinegar and water. Stir until the salt is dissolved. Add the oil and beat until well blended or shake in a jar with a tight lid. Serve at once or beat before serving. Pour over the lettuce and enjoy the tangy salad.

Deviled Eggs

You will need:

Saucepan
Fork
Measuring spoon
Mixing spoon
Small bowl

Recipe:

4 eggs
⅛ teaspoon salt
2 tablespoons mayonnaise
2 teaspoons mustard
1 teaspoon vinegar
  Paprika

Hard-boil the eggs. When the eggs are cool, peel them and cut them in half. Take the yellow center out carefully, put in a bowl and mash with a fork until smooth. Add the vinegar, mustard, mayonnaise, and salt. Mix well. Fill the eight halves with the filling. Place on a plate, sprinkle with paprika, and chill until ready to eat.

Deviled Ham Spread

You will need:

Measuring cup and spoons
Mixing spoon
Spreader
Small bowl

Recipe:

½ cup deviled ham
¼ cup sour cream
 2 tablespoons sweet pickle relish,
      drained
 1 tablespoon grated onion
      Dash tabasco Sauce

Mix all the ingredients together until well
mixed. Serve on crackers, bread, stuffed
in celery, or just plain.

Sour Cream Cucumbers

You will need:

Paring knife
2 small bowls
Mixing spoon

Recipe:

2 medium cucumbers
2 tablespoons lemon juice
½ teaspoon salt
⅛ teaspoon pepper
½ teaspoon paprika
½ small onion, minced
1 cup sour cream

Have the children peel and slice the cucumbers into thin slices. Place in a bowl and chill in the refrigerator or cover with plastic wrap and top with ice cubes. Combine the remaining ingredients in another bowl and blend thoroughly. At serving time, drain any moisture from the cucumber and fold in the dressing for a slightly sour treat salad.

Sour Cream and Cherries

You will need:

Small bowl
Mixing spoon

Recipe:

1 pint sour cream
1 cup cherry jam

Stir the cream and jam together. Chill for 30–45 minutes. This cannot be frozen. This is a tart dessert. Try it in Swedish pancakes or crepes.

Dill Sauce for Fish

You will need:

Measuring cup and spoons
Small bowl
Mixing spoon
Spatula or spreader

Recipe:

2 tablespoons chopped dill
1 teaspoon dill seed
2 tablespoons chopped parsley
2 tablespoons lemon juice
1 teaspoon paprika
½ cup butter, melted
1 teaspoon salt
   Freshly ground pepper
   Halibut, mackerel or salmon

Combine the chopped dill, dill seed, parsley, lemon juice, paprika, salt and pepper with melted butter. Spread half the sauce on one side of the fish and broil for 15 minutes under medium heat. Turn the fish over. Spread the remainder of sauce on the fish and broil for 15 minutes or until done. This will give your fish a tangy taste.

German Potato Salad

You will need:

Potato peeler
Saucepan
Measuring cup and spoons
Skillet
Fork
Paper towel
Paring knife

Recipe:

3 lbs. potatoes (9 medium)
6 slices bacon
¾ cup chopped onion
2 tablespoons flour
2 tablespoons sugar
2 teaspoons salt
½ teaspoon celery seed
   Dash pepper
¾ cup water
⅓ cup vinegar

Wash the potatoes, peel and remove the eyes. Heat one inch salted water (½ teaspoon salt to 1 cup water) to boiling. Add potatoes, cover tightly and heat to a boil. Lower heat and cook 30 to 35 minutes or until tender. Drain and cool.

In a large skillet, fry the bacon until crisp. Remove the bacon and drain on paper towels. Cook and stir the onion in the bacon drippings until tender. Add the flour, sugar, salt, celery seed and pepper, and stir. Cook over a low heat and stir until it bubbles. Remove from the heat, stir in the water and vinegar and bring to a boil, stirring constantly. Boil and stir for one minute.

Crumble the bacon, slice the potatoes thinly and carefully add them to the hot mixture. Heat thoroughly, stirring and lightly coating the potato slices.

Making Sauerkraut

You will need:

Knife
Measuring cup
Colander
Large pot
Mixing spoon

Recipe:

Head of cabbage
Coarse kosher or pickling salt,
    without iodine
Knife
Large bowl
Weight
Plate to cover bowl, or plastic wrap
Cutting board

Cut the cabbage into quarters. Wash and remove the white center core. Thinly shred the cabbage with a knife on the cutting board. Place a layer of cabbage in the bowl and sprinkle with salt. Continue adding layers of cabbage and salt until all the cabbage is used. Put the clean weight on top of the cabbage; then cover with the plate or plastic wrap. Leave the bowl at room temperature for a week. At the end of that time, uncover the cabbage and taste. It should taste like raw sauerkraut. If the taste still resembles cabbage, it needs to ferment longer. Sauerkraut may be eaten raw or cooked.

Cooking Sauerkraut

You will need:

Colander
Large pot
Knife
Stirring spoon

Recipe:

2 cups raw sauerkraut
1 cup beef broth
½ cup cider or peeled sliced apple
1 sliced onion
1 peeled sliced potato
    Caraway seed
    Pepper
    Sausage or frankfurter bits
    (optional)

Drain the sauerkraut in a colander and put in a large pot. Add the beef broth, cider or apple, onion, and caraway seeds to the sauerkraut. If thick sauerkraut is desired, add the potato. Cook for 45 minutes, adding the sausage, frankfurters, or pork bits with the sauerkraut for the last 20 minutes. The combination of the sauerkraut and meat complement each other.

Dill Pickles

You will need:

Quart jars
Bowl
Large pot
Crock or large jar

Recipe:

Fresh pickling cucumbers, 4″ size
    (enough to fill a quart jar ⅔ full).
Dill
Garlic cloves, sliced and peeled
Whole black peppercorns
Bay leaves
Brine mixture: 2 cups salt and 2 cups
    vinegar to every 2 gallons of hot water

Make the brine first. One half as much brine as cucumbers will be needed. Boil the brine in a pot until the salt dissolves.

Wash the cucumbers in cold water. Into the crock, put a layer of cucumbers, then a layer of dill, garlic, and pepper. Add another layer of cucumbers, the seasonings and bay leaf if desired. Continue to add layers until the container is ⅔ full.

Pour the brine over the cucumbers, covering them completely so they will not spoil. Make more brine if necessary. To make certain the cucumbers stay under the brine, put a plate on top of them weighted down with something heavy.

Place the crock of pickles in a warm

place, 65° to 75° F. so they can ferment. Scum will form on top every day, and it must be removed so the pickles will not spoil. A slotted spoon works best.

Fermentation takes two to four weeks. To find out if fermentation has progressed far enough, remove a pickle slice and see if it looks more like a pickle than a cucumber.

When the pickles are ready to your liking, pack them into clean quart jars without the brine. Boil the brine once more before pouring it over the pickles again. These pickles will keep safely in the refrigerator for a month.

Sourdough Starter

You will need:

Measuring cup and spoon
Bowl
Stirring spoon

Recipe:

1 package dry yeast
2 cups flour
1 cup warm water
1 teaspoon sugar
  Cup, bowl, or jar with a lid

Three days before you plan to bake the sourdough bread, you must prepare a sourdough starter. Mix the yeast, 1 cup of flour and water together in a bowl, cup, or jar. Cover the container and keep it in a warm place (the top of the refrigerator is a good place) for two days. The mixture should bubble up and really smell yeasty. If nothing has happened, stir in a teaspoon of sugar and make sure the container is in a warm place. This should revive the mixture. Let it multiply for two more days. When it is ready, store in the refrigerator to keep it dormant until needed.

The day before you bake, remove the starter from the refrigerator and add the second cup of flour and a cup of warm water to double the mixture. Leave the yeast out so it can multiply. Half of this mixture will be used for the baking and the other half will be saved for the next time.

Sourdough Bread

You will need:

Large bowl
Bread board
Towel
Cookie sheet

Recipe:

2 cups starter (put the remainder
   back in the refrigerator)
2 tablespoons melted butter
1 tablespoon sugar
1 teaspoon salt
2½–3 cups regular flour
   Butter to grease the bowl

Mix all the ingredients except for the melted butter in a large bowl. (Start with 2½ cups of flour. If the dough is too sticky to make into a ball, add more flour. On a floured board or table, turn out the dough and knead it until it is smooth, elastic, and slightly glossy.

Rinse out the bowl; then grease it with some butter and put the dough into the bowl, turning it over so both sides have butter on them. Cover the dough with a damp kitchen towel and put it in a warm place. In about an hour, the dough should be twice its original size.

Flour the board again and put the dough on the board. Give it some punches to make it small again. Knead for 2 to 3 minutes; then divide the dough into two

153

parts and shape each part into a loaf of bread of any shape. If the dough is too elastic to work with, let it rise for ten more minutes and shape into loaves.

Slash patterns across the top of the loaves—crosses, diamonds, or any other pattern. These slits should be ½″ deep. (These prevent the loaves of bread from splitting as they rise.)

Place the loaves on a cookie sheet and cover them with a damp towel. Let them rise until they are double in size. This should take less than an hour. Preheat the oven to 400°.

Bake the bread for ten minutes at 400° to get a good crust; then turn the oven to 375° and bake until the bread is golden brown. Check them at 30 minutes and re-check until done. Remove from the oven, cool slightly, then enjoy.

Bitter Recipes

Olive and Pimento Cheese Sandwich

You will need:

Knife
Spreader

Recipe:

Pimento cheese spread
Stuffed green olives
Choice of bread

Spread one slice of bread with pimento cheese and arrange sliced stuffed olives on top. Cover with another slice of bread. This sandwich will have a bitter taste.

Cucumber and Radish Sandwich

You will need:

Knife
Spreader

Recipe:

Whole wheat bread
Butter or mayonnaise
Cucumber
Radishes
Lemon juice
Salt

Spread the bread with butter or mayonnaise. Slice the cucumber and radishes thinly. Place a layer of cucumbers and then a layer of radishes on top of a slice of bread. Sprinkle the top with lemon juice and salt. The radishes will give this sandwich a slightly bitter taste.

Brussels Sprouts

You will need:

Knife
Saucepan with lid

Recipe:

Brussels sprouts
Water
Salt

Remove any discolored leaves and cut off the stems. Heat 1″ salted water to a boil (½ teaspoon salt to 1 cup of water). Add the Brussels sprouts; cover and bring to boil. Cook 8–10 minutes or until tender. Drain and serve with butter, salt, and pepper; or seasoned with garlic salt, basil, caraway seed, cumin, dill, marjoram, sage or savory salt; or creamed; or topped with cheese sauce.

Dips for All Tastes

You will need:

Small bowl
Mixing spoon
Fork

Basic dip recipe:

1 8-oz. package cream cheese
   Cream, milk, or sour cream
   Choice of flavorings, additions, and
     things to dip with from the lists
     in the instructions

Take the cream cheese out of the refrigerator and let it stand until it reaches room temperature. Soften it by stirring it with a fork; then thin it by adding a small amount of cream, milk, or sour cream. Mix with spoon until smooth. You can decide the consistency of the dip.

Add one or more of the following to flavor your dip mixture:
   Worchestershire sauce
   Garlic or onion salt
   Horseradish
   Chives
   Parsley
   Mustard
   Soy sauce
   Dill
   Basil
   Other herbs
   Curry powder

Paprika
Ginger
Other spices
Chili powder
Dry salad dressing mixes

From the following suggestions, chop up and add one or more things which will complement the flavored dip mix.
Onions or scallions
Nuts
Olives
Anchovies
Deviled ham
Cooked clams
Fried bacon
Salami
Pimentos
Blue cheese
Tuna fish
Ortega chilis

Select from the following list one or more kinds of things to dip with:
Corn chips
Potato chips
Tortilla chips
Cheese crackers
Carrot
Celery
Cauliflower
Cucumber
Cherry tomato
Broccoli stems
Zucchini
String beans
Radishes
Crackers
Melba toast
Other raw vegetables